WEEKEND WOODWORKING FOR KIDS, TEENS AND PARENTS:

A Beginner's Guide with 20 DIY Projects for Digital Detox and Family Bonding

Stephen Fleming

Bonus Booklet

Thanks for purchasing the book. In addition to the content, we are also providing an additional booklet consisting of a Monthly Planner and Project Schedule template for your first project.

It contains valuable information about woodworking and leathercraft.

Download the booklet by typing the below link.

http://bit.ly/leatherbonus

Cheers!

Word of Caution

Woodworking can turn dangerous, as I've personally seen and heard about many unfortunate accidents; therefore, the utmost priority should be given to safety and security while practicing this rewarding and creative activity.

Specifically, I'll share all my experiences in this book, but it's essential to remember that woodworking is naturally risky, just like various other kinds of practices.

Failure to use devices and tools appropriately or not adhering to recommended safety standards could result in significant injury.

In other words, it's your sole responsibility to ensure that you fully understand your tools and devices and how to use them properly before attempting a woodworking task.

Thoroughly read, recognize, and adhere to your tools or devices' most current guidelines and safety precautions.

Any book, video, or other learning means can't replace learning physically from an expert. These forms of information offer only additional guidance for usage with practical demonstration and training from an experienced woodworker.

Kids and teens should practice it strictly under adult supervision, and a first aid kit should be kept nearby in case of any cut.

All the projects mentioned reflect my unique way of doing it. Yet, the same projects can be executed differently by other woodcrafters. So use any technique at your own risk.

In sum, the first and foremost tip is to wear all the safety equipment and follow protective guidelines every time you practice woodworking. The author isn't responsible in any way for an injury caused by practicing woodworking.

<u>Few Clarifications</u>

- The Parent/Guardian or the adult overseeing and guiding the Kid/Teen must have basic level experience using woodworking tools.

- The essential list of tools mentioned would be required. (The best way to start is to join any offline class/training where the tools are already available. After that, decide which one to buy.)

- The project mentioned also requires using electrical tools. I recommend only adults to use them. The kids can at most use the manual tools, that too based on the judgment of Parent/Guardian or the adult overseeing and guiding the Kid/Teen.

- The main aim is to involve the Parents and Kids/Teens in doing something creative and spending quality time.

- Most of the complicated work would be done by the adult, and the kids/teen would perform limited simple activities and then learn by observation.

- Any publication, video, or other ways of learning can't replace live training or class. These kinds of information offer only extra assistance along with practical demonstration and training from an experienced woodworker.

Table of Contents

<u>Chapter Name</u>	**<u>Pg. No.</u>**
1. About Woodworking & Wood	7-14
2. Woodworking for Kids & Teens	15-23
3. Tools, Processes, and Techniques	24-42
4. Woodworking Safety	43-46
5. Beginner Projects	47-103
6. Final Tips and Conclusion	104-108
7. Appendix	109-114

PREFACE

Are you a parent looking for ways to engage with your kids and teens, bond with them, and have fun?

Are you looking for ways to help turn off the smartphones, tablets, and television and still have your kids and teens occupied with a fun, creative, and collaborative activity?

In an ever-changing society, there aren't a whole lot of activities that are geared towards children, teens, and parents. Marketing strategies have become so specific that they target the same age ranges. s

Fortunately, if you take a step back from "modern" society, you can get involved in some age-old crafts and practical skills that are engaging and rewarding for the whole family!

Woodworking is such a craft. Not only are there projects that range in difficulty for different skill and age groups, but there are some projects that can be completed by two people, giving you a chance to interact and bond with your children and teens face to face. Without the input of noise and visual stimulation from screen entertainment, you and your family members can talk to each other and create something memorable together.

Woodworking is a detail-oriented craft, so it is best to unplug entirely, removing distractions like phones and screened devices while participating. It's a good excuse for you and your children to step back and develop a diverse set of skills. An experienced instructor passionately exclaimed: **"Working with wood clears obstructions of learning in kids."**

By utilizing this book, you'll learn about mandatory woodworking skills. You'll master essential techniques and be introduced to the proper tools and materials for the crafts. Additionally, you'll explore several projects with step by step instructions to get started on with your children and teens. This is a great place to start digital detox and bonding activities!

Stephen Fleming

Chapter 1: About Woodworking and Wood

> An experienced Woodworker once said to me, "There is no scrap wood, just pieces which have not met the right hand".

I always believe that real learning starts with definitions of the core of the craft. Here, in this case, it's wood and the craft of woodworking. So below are the descriptions of major types of woodworking and wood.

Woodworking:

Woodworking is the activity or skill of making items from wood and includes *cabinet making (cabinetry and furniture), wood carving, joinery, carpentry, and woodturning.*

Cabinet Making: This is the art of making wooden cabinets through woodworking skills and tools.

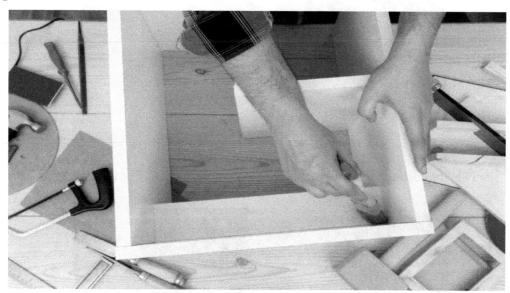

Cabinet Making

Wood Carving: This is a form of woodworking that involves sculpting figurines or decorative wooden pieces by carving the wood with a chisel and a mallet.

Depicted below include the various types of wood carving:

Whittling   In-The-Round-Carving

Relief Carving   Chip Carving

Joinery: Joinery is the technique through which two or more pieces of timber are attached.

Examples of Joinery

Carpentry: Carpentry is related to cutting, shaping, and installing wood frames/structures in building, bridges, ships, etc. So, it's associated with the wooden frames used in the construction industry today.

Carpenter

Woodturning: In woodturning, an item of wood is placed onto a lathe, which rotates the wood quickly. As it spins, the woodworker uses tools such as cuts and blades to delicately cut away at the turning wood to shape it as well as form a pattern of grooves

Woodturning

About Wood:

Types of wood you'll likely encounter:
1. Hardwoods
2. Softwoods
3. Plywood
4. MDF

Softwood:

When you go to a residential facility or lumberyard, the chances are that the fragrance you detect is pine.

Green Pine

This is one of the most common woods you can purchase and is also typically the most budget-friendly. Pine boards are used in house construction and framework. They're perfect for tasks that you plan to paint; however, many people like the unpainted natural appearances as well.

#	Hardwood	Softwood
durability	Highly durable and lasts for several decades	Less durable
color	Darkly colored wood	Usually lightly colored wood
weight	Heavyweight with a rough texture	Lightweight with a fine texture
fiber	Fibers are close and dense	Less fiber
source	Hardwood is collected from deciduous trees	Softwood is collected from evergreen trees

Hardwood

When you think about fine furnishings and traditional woodworking, you may imagine wood varieties such as mahogany, walnut, or cherry. Primarily, people buy hardwoods due to their grain pattern, color, or longevity.

If you want to develop something that lasts hundreds of years, hardwood is an excellent option. Hardwood is rarely tarnished as well, as this would be a waste of money to cover it up with paint. It's usually shielded with a clear coating, such as varnish, lacquer, or oil.

Softwood   Hardwood

Hardwoods are excellent for integrating different styles by utilizing other wood. Walnut and maple, for instance, are commonly seen on chess boards.

The thickness of hardwoods can make them tough on devices, and they can be challenging to shape. Less-than-sharp table saw blades are notorious for leaving shed marks on cherry and maple, thus calling for a great deal of sanding.

The biggest disadvantage is that hardwoods can be costly – particularly more unique types. It may be challenging even to find hardwood lumber where you live. Fortunately, there are online hardwood sellers that will certainly select the best boards to ship to you.

Oak offers one of the most common and affordable hardwoods in the U.S., and together with maple and walnut, oak is typically available at most relevant stores. Oak has its issues, but it looks good and is a terrific starter choice.

Plywood

Plywood is among the most popular and most versatile building materials you can use. It can be one of the most confusing, as there are so many grades with their coded designations.

Plywood in the woodshop

You can do a Google search for Plywood Grades to read more on this subject. Plywood varies because it's made artificially. Thin veneers of genuine wood are piled in contrary grain and glued together. This crisscrossing is what gives plywood its stamina as well as security.

As a whole, the more layers, the higher the quality. Plywood that comes fine sanded on both sides is the best. It's also wise to seek the plywood with the least amount of space along the edge.

You can also purchase specialized maple, oak, cherry, or other hardwood plywood. These are often on the pricier side.

There's absolutely nothing wrong with saving money by purchasing lesser quality plywood for store projects, jigs, or fixtures. It's a mostly visual difference.

Less expensive plywood is rough and knotty, but it can be useful for many jobs that don't need a pretty end product, such as shop tasks.

Why use plywood?

There are a lot of advantages to plywood versus solid lumber. Firstly, it's reasonably affordable. Also, plywood is solid and steady: you don't need to stress over-expansion as well as tightening. It won't warp. It's a fantastic option for large surfaces, such as a tabletop.

Drawbacks of Plywood

There are a couple of negative aspects of using plywood. A 4'x 8's sheet of plywood is heavy and difficult to move and manage alone for one person. Nevertheless, many home centers can cut it into smaller pieces for you. Steering a complete sheet of plywood can be a challenge.

Second, while the face of the plywood looks excellent, the edges can be an eyesore. You can cover these up with iron-on edge banding or make your very own side banding out of solid timber. If you're feeling a little uncertain, just welcome the split appearance and use it as a layout element!

A great trick is to run some concealing tape along your cut line when cutting against the grain. Also, make use of a sharp blade. We're using concealing tape to prevent chip-out when crossing the grain on plywood.

MDF

Lastly, I want to speak briefly about **Medium Density Fiberboard**, or MDF, made by pressing wood fibers into boards. It's not to everyone's taste, but it is economical and valuable in some tasks. MDF is commonly used in knockdown furniture, like what you may need to assemble from IKEA or other stores. It's typically laminated or coated. The material itself is easy to work with, as it cuts like butter. It's an excellent choice for small or ornamental indoor projects that you will paint. Also, you don't need to stress over splintering.

MDF

Drawbacks of MDF

MDF can be a little fragile, particularly near the edges where it can collapse like cardboard if you aren't cautious. The faces are solid. If you use it for racks longer than 2 feet or so, they'll ultimately sag. It's likewise heavy: a full-size sheet isn't easy to move on your own.

MDF can be vulnerable around the edges. This split can be stopped by simply drilling a hole initially.

However, the most significant disadvantage to MDF is the fine dirt it produces when you sand it. It's certainly not something you want to breathe: wear a respirator and have a dust collection mechanism connected to your tools.

For starters, you can use free wood. Craigslist is a fantastic source for individuals giving away free lumber. Likewise, if you don't mind a little additional work, think about getting wood from old pallets. I've broken down plenty of free oak pallets. Above all, have fun, and don't hesitate to try something brand-new!

Trying out a small saw on cardboard first

2. Woodworking for Kids & Teens

> **"Woodwork is not about what children make – it's about the changes that are made within the child"** - *Pete Moorhouse*

Kids in their early years may have very different future professions that don't exist yet.

It's more crucial than ever for the new generation to think creatively and develop problem-solving abilities.

Woodworking teaches such skills as children make their selections and discover via experimentation.

It stimulates creativity and imagination, qualities that are as important as the functional skills acquired. Woodwork ensures the connection between all facets of learning and development.

Initially, children & teens are shown how to safely utilize the devices and offered a chance to attempt strategies in the right ways. As they gain mastery, joy, and also satisfaction, it provides their self-worth a visible boost. Once they've grasped basic skills, they engage in open-ended inquiry, making notable developments.

In the process, their imagination, creativity, and also analytical skills prosper as they meet and conquer their very own difficulties. I've observed just how woodwork encourages independence as youngsters develop their own solutions to obstacles that emerge.

I hope this book will certainly provide you confidence and practical knowledge to introduce kids and teens to woodworking.

Why should kids learn woodworking?

Children working with wood pieces are developing qualities and skills to face adult life challenges.

Several people are amazed by the idea of kids working with real tools.

Choosing the wood piece

Still, the woodwork has a history in early youth education and learning since Froebel's Preschool days. It practically vanished in current decades, but it's now making a comeback, with a restored rate of interest from all around the world. A silent revolution is happening!

There's something unique regarding woodwork. It's so different from various other tasks. The odor and also feel of wood, using real devices, collaborating with a natural material, the noises of hammering and sawing, and the fusion of hands and minds collaborating to reveal their imagination and fix issues. Besides, it encourages stamina as well as coordination: all incorporated to obtain kids' interest. It provides a unique experience.

However, what about safety and security?

Woodwork could be a low-risk task as long as some necessary precautions are taken and suitable devices are utilized.

I observed that kids' focus improves at the woodwork bench-- they're wholly involved and do something they appreciate.

Likewise, it's important that children experience threats and challenges within a controlled environment, so they learn to make their own decisions and judgments to safeguard themselves. This is a crucial facet of child and adolescent development.

Woodwork is a terrific tool for expressive art and also an innovative layout.

It also involves many other subjects of learning and advancement, giving a truly cross-curricular task. Mathematical reasoning is developed, scientific knowledge is obtained, technological understanding is established via dealing with tools, and kids become engineers as they create.

Woodwork is an outstanding art form for establishing youngsters' creative and essential thinking skills and encourages them to experiment with the possibilities of timber and tools.

Woodwork has a considerable influence on youngsters' self-worth and self-confidence and establishes a sense of company-- that "can-do" attitude.

Woodwork is a medium for kids to express their imagination as well as creativity.

It's important to give tasks where the kids and teens use their imaginations and don't merely copy the project. There should be some personalization from their side, which would make it unique.

The key to children remaining engrossed in woodwork is that they follow their own passions and solve their own problems to create their projects. The project becomes more meaningful when it has been initiated and is led by youngsters.

Initially, their job is usually totally experimental-- dabbling with the possibilities of the products and tools. Children then reveal their imagination in a range of creative means by generating projects they deem interesting.

The procedures involved in woodwork create youngsters' expertise in building and construction. In woodwork, they'll inevitably join as well as build in a selection of various ways. They find that timber sections with level sides are less complicated to link than tilted pieces. They discover how to make joins solid and durable or how to make their design stand up.

Woodwork with little ones gives excellent structure in main and secondary education directly linked to all the STEM (Science, Technology, Engineering, and Mathematics) subjects. To truly allow youngsters to recognize these ideas, we must offer genuine real experiences, not abstract alternatives. With hands-on learning, children construct a foundation in their learning, acquiring practical skills like decision making and problem-solving.

Therefore, once more, woodwork could be seen as an essential subject/skill that can train your child or teen for creative and analytical hands-on applications at the same time.

Suggestions for parents and family members

As a parent, I can suggest taking your time and starting slowly when woodworking with your kids or teens! Implementing woodworking does not imply beginning with a complete set of hand tools power tools.

Practice and teach woodworking to your kids in a straightforward manner. Start with sandpaper and wood; and a tiny rubber mallet (Minimal tools).

Father-son duo practicing woodworking

From there, you can introduce an item like a screwdriver.

Present one tool and also one skill at a time.

Let children and teens learn about wood-- keep in mind the grain, the scent, the structures, the weight, differences in types, etc.

Show the kids just how to utilize actual devices correctly.

Make it clear that if children don't adhere to the security policies, they'll certainly need to leave that area and play somewhere else.

Security is always the number one priority! This principle can be instructed, as can healthy respect for tools.

Children (ages 5 and up) may be utilizing real tools. (The little plastic workbench is appropriate for youngsters 4 and below.)

There are collections of genuine child-size tools for around $20-$50 at Home Depot. Determine the appropriate names of every one of the devices before telling your kids.

Trace the overview of the devices on the pegboard for children to place the devices back when they're finished with them. Goggles/eyewear should always be put on.

 In case you use a saw if, make sure it's attached to the workbench to hold the wood in place while sawing.

The best-suited wood for kids and beginners is softwoods-- white pine, cedar, fir, and redwood. Lumber companies, cabinetmakers, karate schools, and equipment stores, if asked, frequently will certainly give away scraps of timber.

You can start the nails for youngsters. You can additionally place a comb between the nail head and also the child's fingers as an obstacle to prevent injury.

The woodworking area needs to be well supervised at all times!

Safety and security are critical!!!

Benefits of woodworking for kids and teens

Woodworking is a preferred hobby for families, especially parents, kids, and teens, who can practice some simple woodworking projects together.

Parents and children can work on a project and communicate from start to end, making memories of good times. The children can practice numerous recommended beginner-friendly wood tasks to spend their free time on weekends or holidays.

Kid checking the wood piece

Woodworking activity is very beneficial for kids and teens as it helps to inculcate and grow the following skills:

- Eye-hand synchronization

- Motor Skills

- Problem-solving

- Role-playing

- Creative thinking

- Independence/self-esteem

- Stress and anxiety reducer

- Matching and classification.

- Sorting/Pattern Analysis

20

- Comparing/measuring

- Cooperation/Teamwork

- Respect for tools and products.

- Communication

As cited in ***Adams and Taylor, 1982,*** there are seven stages of woodworking learning for children:

(Reference: Adams, P. & Taylor, M. (1982). Children's workshops: ideas for carpentry centers)

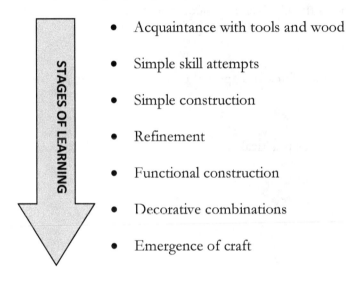

- Acquaintance with tools and wood

- Simple skill attempts

- Simple construction

- Refinement

- Functional construction

- Decorative combinations

- Emergence of craft

Stage 1: Acquaintance with tools and wood

It's vital to gain preliminary exposure to tools and woods via a range of uses such as physical qualities, weight, structure, equilibrium, toughness, etc.

Phase 2: Simple skill attempts

Throughout this phase, kids can actively discover the abilities associated with tools like hammering, sawing, utilizing screwdrivers, timber adhesive, etc.

Phase 3: Easy Constructions

As youngsters become extra comfortable with the use of the tools, they begin to try new projects. They also start to strategy, sequence, trouble address, and also create new ideas. For instance, forms and various other designs are developed with numerous items.

Phase 4: Refinement

The kids continue to explore as well as acquire confidence in the woodworking location by doing beginner projects. They start to improve or add finishing touches to their tasks such as sanding, painting, or creating uses.

Stage 5: Functional construction

Now the project looks more realistic as the children put pieces together to form a shape.

Phase 6: Decorative combinations

In this stage, children use various combinations and apply their creativity for unique results.

Stage 7: Appearance of Craft

The skills discovered are employed both as practical and symbolic ability. Children will try new ideas and fine-tune existing techniques.

Safety Checklist

- Always use safety glasses.

- Be consistent when delivering correct instruction to kids and teens on the appropriate use of all devices.

- Sawing-- Wood should always be clamped when being sawn. An adult must stand in front of the sawing area to avoid anyone getting near the saw. After usage, the saw should be quickly kept in a safe place. Japanese saw: a kid should hold the saw with two hands. Western saw: A youngster should hold the saw with one hand; the other hand should be far away and holding the bench.

- Wood: Avoid hardwoods, plywood, and also treated wood. Don't cut MDF due to extreme dust.

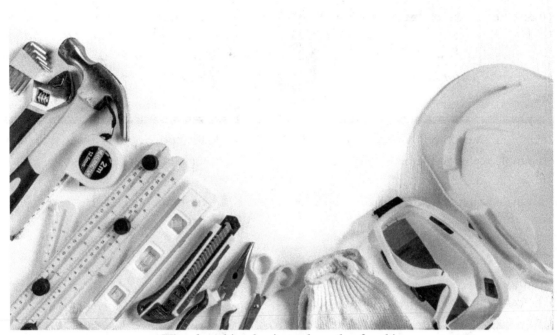

Woodworking basic tools and safety kit

- Eliminate protruding nails from completed items.

- Maintain the flooring clear to protect against tripping.

- Avoid splintery timber.

- Set up a particular workspace to stop disturbances.

- Keep an emergency treatment and first aid kit available

3. Tools, Processes, and Techniques

> *"Woodwork is an effective tool for establishing youngster's innovative thought process, as well as critical thinking. There are countless chances for youngsters to resolve complicated issues as well as express their infinite creative imagination."- A Woodworking Instructor*

When you buy power tools, think about getting the latest tools and systems that work off a compatible rechargeable battery.

This ensures that there's no cord to trip over, and also, the tools are portable.

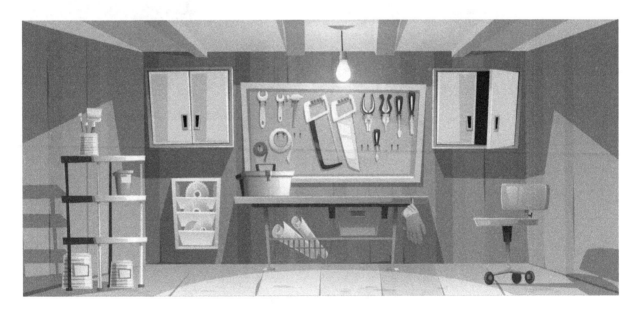

Woodworking workspace with tools

Safety Tip:

Educate your kid to be mindful when carrying devices. She/he always needs to hold the sharp sides or point downward and away from the body. When handing a device to more than one individual, transfer the handle first.

If you have to work with timber regularly, you'll need some devices. Much of these tools can be found in any basic home repair service device kit, so they're not something you have to acquire, especially for this craft:

- Metal tape measure

| Tape | Ruler | Crosscut saw |

- Ruler

- Sharp pencil

- Pliers

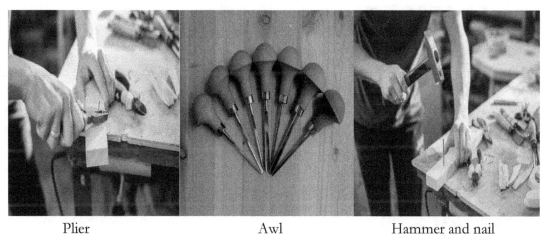

| Plier | Awl | Hammer and nail |

- Pencil compass

- Crosscut saw

- Awl

- Safety glasses.

- Hammer

- Toenail

- Nails.

- Screws

- Screwdrivers

- Hand drill

- Glue /adhesive

- Vise (These are jaws used to hold a wood piece without denting it.)

Vise   Power Tools

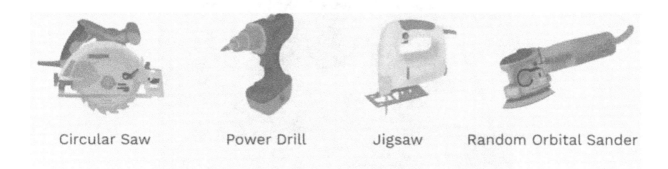

Circular Saw   Power Drill   Jigsaw   Random Orbital Sander

- Sandpaper (in numerous grades)

Some power devices you might seek that you'll utilize on your own (or oversee an older child or teen with) are:

- Power drill for piercing or to drive screws right into wood or remove them.

- Circular/Round saw for cutting timber.

- Power sander for finishing timber and also planning for paint or stain.

Don't consider buying low-grade tools for your child if you're in any way serious about creating a passion for woodworking or carpentry.

Instead, get top quality tools you can adjust to a kid's usage. For example, screwdrivers can be found in various handgrip sizes. Buy some with a much shorter handle so your youngster can hold them quickly. Let the kid or teen utilize a hammer for driving little nails. (You may need to drive bigger nails with a full-sized hammer until your younger child can grip a full-sized claw hammer.) Don't presume youngsters can't utilize a device until you show them how and give them a chance to practice.

Power Sander

Once a friend of mine asked, tell me 8 primary tools, I should teach my kids to use. Well, below summarizes my choice for initial tools for kids based on my experience:

1. Screwdrivers

Screws can assist in binding several beginner joints. Also, the kid should know about the differences between screws.

2. Tape Measure

Gauging furniture around your house is an excellent method to discover just how to read a measuring tape.

3. Block Plane

A small block plane isn't likely to be a store workhorse for a child, yet they'll genuinely appreciate making use of one. Making shavings is something grownups enjoy, and kids are no different.

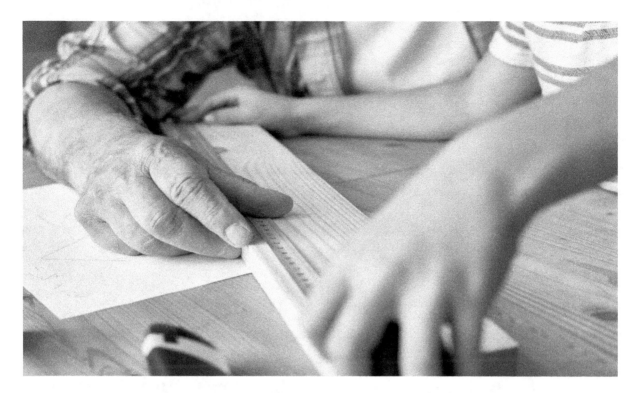

Measuring wood

4. Clamps

Clamps are handy for all woodworkers (adults or kids), from safeguarding a piece a child is working on to putting together a newly developed joint; clamps are as helpful to kids as they are to adults. It is essential to learn the types of clamps and their usability as per the project type.

5. Vise

Like clamps, a vise is essential to hold a surface while it's being worked upon. Little hands aren't stable, and a vise makes a challenging operation a lot easier.

6. Cordless Drill

The initial power device, a low-powered, tiny drill, is handy in drilling pilot holes, countersinking, using dowels as well as driving screws.

7. Hammer

A hammer is a straightforward device, as well as it can be used with nails, assembly, touching in dowels, and a lot more. A small hammer is best, and also can be discovered at lots of equipment shops.

8. Hand Saw

Japanese saw is what I always trust with myself and my kids. Keep the same type of saw and maintain the continuity for better adaption.

Steps /Process towards woodworking:

Setting up the woodworking area

The first step to choose is a suitable place. Select a location where there aren't many distractions as children can lose focus while sawing or hammering.

Woodworking area

I prefer a corner area, and if that isn't available, storage space racks can be placed to avoid cross movement in that area.

Doing woodwork outdoors is fantastic. Nonetheless, cold weather can be repulsive, and put on several layers of clothes limits body movement. A workbench is necessary for sawing wood. Devices can be conveniently depending upon your setting as well as on what jobs best for your children.

Selecting Wood

There's no alternative to balsa timber to start with. It's so soft as well as effortless to hammer into that youngsters rapidly get confidence; in a snap, they'll soon be knocking in nail after nail.

Balsa is additionally perfect for learning to screw and saw. It's costly, so it is best kept for these initial stages. When traditional skills are learned, children can move to other soft timbers: pine, cedar, fir, larch, redwood, poplar, lime, and spruce.

Pine is one of the most easily found woods. Check if the wood is soft enough by seeing if you can indent it a little with your fingernail. Search for sustainably grown wood; these ways, you're not contributing to logging and always have a supply. Softwoods can be purchased from any type of wood seller; however, you can probably get sufficient offcuts from moms and dads and neighborhood woodworkers or builders.

Softwood pieces ready to be worked upon

While presenting woodworking to a kid or teen, the initial sessions may emphasize tools, skills, and confidence.

Introduction to tools

Start with children sitting at a low working table. This enables them to take their time and investigate at their own rate. When dealing with an older kid, demonstrate just how to make use of the hammer and screwdriver.

First, we learn to make use of the hammer. Some kids are anxious at first but will quickly knock in their first number of nails. Thus, their fulfillment is evident as they persistently pound in one after another.

Start with 1-inch or 25mm round nails. Then move by using a screw and also joining technique. These two skills help starter projects, as kids get inspired to make airplanes and so on.

We start with small screws. Number 8 or 10s, 3/4 inch long, make the task relativity easy so strengthen children's self-confidence.

A kid learning to use a hammer

Always use crosshead screws as they're most convenient. After that, present the drill and also the G clamps. Explain to them the usage and best practices of tools. Explain that the tools need to be returned to a designated place after use.

Tools for kids:

You'll certainly require a standard toolkit consisting of hammers, screwdrivers, saws, hand drills, clamps, numbers of nails, and screws.

New tools can be added to youngsters' toolkits as per increasing abilities.

Having the right devices makes a significant difference. For example, a short-handled hammer with a large head, excellent grip, and practical weight is superb for kids, whereas a long-handled pin hammer is challenging to use.

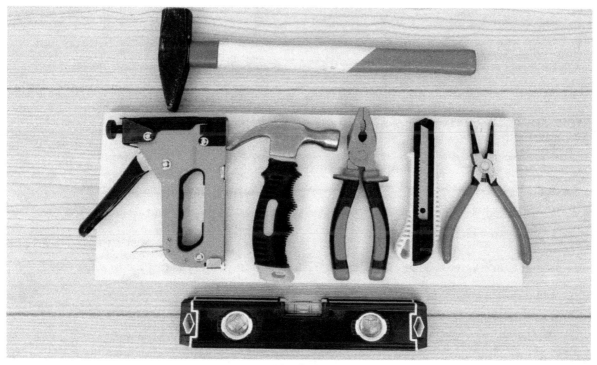

Tool Set

Suggested Tools:

- Wooden Workbench
- Stubby Ball Pein Hammer
- Pistol grip hand drill

- Device box saw
- Japanese saw
- Shatterproof glass
- Short stubby hammers
- Battery screwdriver
- Hexagonal drill little bits
- Tape measures/rulers
- Wood adhesive
- Sandpaper
- Short stubby screwdriver
- Saw
- G clamps
- Nails, screws, nuts, bolts
- Wrenches
- Spanners
- Pliers
- Hand drill
- Drill bits

Setting up a workspace:

1. Workbench

Giving a dedicated workbench for carpentry isn't required at home, but a kid warrants a table surface area of some kind.

A workbench is necessary to guarantee that all devices and timber are kept together.

2. Wood

Having a variety of wood and an adequate supply is essential for kids' selection and creativity. Workshops, some hardware shops, building organizations, tree-cutters, and sawmills can give off-cuts free.

Branches that are 5 cm to 10cm thick can be excellent for sawing and easy to find. House clearance businesses commonly have broken tables they want to give away, given that they have no worth. Pallets are typically totally free, and with a lever and a hammer, they can be worked upon.

3. Vices and also clamps

Youngsters don't have the stamina to hold a piece of wood and cut with one hand like a grown-up, so the first step is to show them how to use a vice or G-clamp to hold the wood still.

Vices can be purchased from hardware shops and need to be bolted to the bench so they don't move. Designer's vices are preferable as they're a lot easier to attach to the workbench and prevent the threat of youngsters' sawing into the benchtop. Or a great choice is a couple of G clamp vices since they're economical.

4. Saws

Utilizing a saw is rather difficult when all you understand is that you're required to push it back and forth as quickly and as forcefully as you can. This technique is dangerous. A sheet of plywood behind the saw as a backstop is terrific and will prevent any injury in case the kid slides.

The best method to start sawing is to have the child follow a pencil line or mark on the wood's top.

Put the saw on the marked line. Next, with a little force, draw the saw in reverse. After that, put the saw on once again and draw it backward. As soon as a groove of around 5mm has been developed, get the child or teen to lightly press the saw forwards and backward till the groove is around 2cm deep.

5. Pliers

Pliers are generally utilized for pulling and picking things. Pliers are relatively similar to scissors, and the kid gets used to using them like tongs to choose items up.

Avoid having pliers with cutters, as these can be unsafe if a finger obtains captured. Small digital pliers are the best size for children and are readily available. These have to do with half the dimension of design pliers and a better fit for little hands.

6. Hammers as well as nails

Adults may be afraid that if they allow children to have hammers, then the youngsters will hit each other. However, just as there's a risk, kids will hit each other with various other items such as blocks from the block edge or spades from the sandpit. It's a situation of guidance, viewing kids, and seeing that hammers (and various other tools) are used for the specific purposes planned.

For security factors, talk with children regarding raising the hammer no higher than their head elevation-- this prevents them from accidentally hitting themselves or one more youngster behind them.

Tiny or child-sized hammers can be purchased from equipment stores. Reducing a normal size wooden-handled hammer is an affordable and basic exercise, requiring only a routine saw.

Show and also explain to kids about utilizing your wrist and swinging the hammer to hit the nail. When the kid has actually gained confidence in operating the much shorter hammer, he or she can begin holding the nail alone to get started.

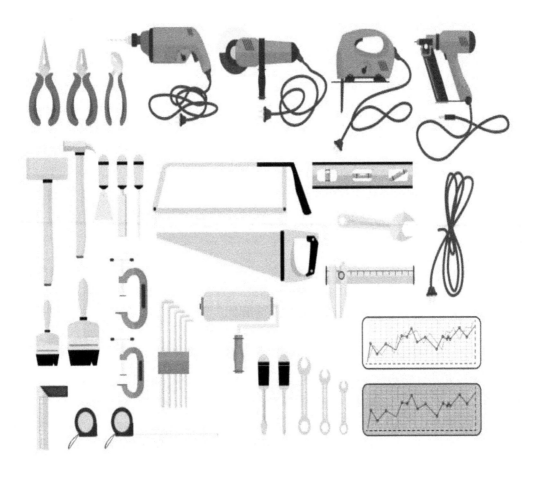

Manual and Electrical Woodworking Tools

Basic Hand Tools

- **Workbench:** A wooden workbench is the key tool of a woodworker's workshop. If you're really on a tight budget, using clamps to secure your work surface is an excellent replacement for various other tools.

  I'd further recommend that you either construct a wooden workbench or purchase one if you don't feel capable. Whichever you choose, you need a robust wooden workbench with at least three durable tops, stable, helpful base legs, and at least one strong vice.

Kids' workbench adjusted to his height

- **Jack Plane& Block Plane:**

  A jackplane is an intermediate-sized "bench plane."If you're on a tight budget; a jackplane can momentarily be used instead of various other planes that have more specialized functions:
- rough supply removal

- jointing board sides
- smoothing the boards

Jack Plane   Block Plane

Block Plane: These little planes can be used to trim your joints, put chamfers on edges, trim end grain, etc. I'd recommend a low-angle block plane, as the reduced angle allows you to cut difficult grain much more quickly.

- **Rabbet Plane:** Rabbets are among the most common joints in furniture production, so a hand plane that cuts a rabbet must be at the top of your purchase list. Yes, rabbets can be cut without a hand plane. However, it's more challenging.

- **Coping Saw:** This cost-effective tool is used regularly for rough cutting shapes on the board, particularly for removing waste from dovetail joints (among one of the most common wooden joints). A cost-effective coping saw will work fine, along with a pack of budget-friendly, extra blades.

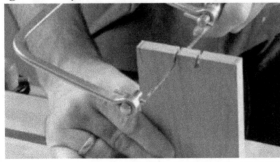

Coping Saw   Hand Saw

- **Panel Saw**: Handsaws (usually called "panel saws") are long, thin saws with a comfortable wooden handle. They're utilized for the harsh dimensioning of your lumber. Although a "panel saw" is technically a smaller handsaw that fits into the panel of a device chest, from this point, I'll refer to this type of saw as a "panel saw" to separate it from the broad classification of "hand saws."Panel saws are made with two tooth setups: "rip" and cross-cut." You'll certainly need both.

- **Miter Box and Saw**: An excellent miter box & miter saw (a very large backsaw) will allow for cutting the exact right length at the right angles. They'll save you a great deal of time when attempting to square your board finishes. The lengthy miter saw glides through a rigid saw frame.

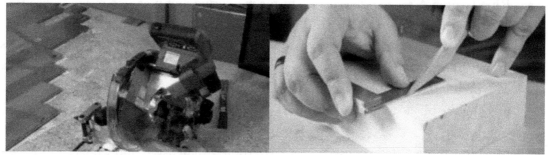

Miter Saw   Marking Knife

- **Marking Knife:** This is used for keeping where you'll be cutting with your saw or chisel. For challenging situations (like dovetails) and making very straight lines (which is crucial for tight-fitting joints), you need the perfect marking knife.

- **Chisel:** A chisel is one of the most common tools you will come across. A premium-quality collection of bevel side bench chisels (new or vintage) will last you several years (maybe even your whole life) as well as be useful in virtually every project. I've made use of some affordable plastic grip bench chisels, although I do favor lighter wooden handle chisels with exceptional steel.

- **Tape Measure/Folding Rule**: A "folding rule" (not "ruler") comes before a tape measure and enables you to measure dimensions when cutting boards, etc. If you're on a limited budget, a little tape measure can be used again and again.

Chisel   Tape Measure

- **Rule Guide:** A metal rule is excellent for measuring, but it can be tough to use for a design job. The trouble is the density of the rule itself. It creates a "step" between the surface area and the workpiece, which can make moving a mark less than accurate. You can use a tiny timber block that makes it easier to mark a line, in this case, accurately. You just align the end of the block with the preferred increment on the rule. After that, note the line by utilizing the block as a rule guide.

- **Marking gauge**: This is used for transferring a dimension and duplicating it. A locking mechanism stops the gauge from slipping and you from loosing that measurement. You can't effectivcly create furniture without an efficient and sturdy marking gauge.

Marking Gauge

- **Combination Square, Try Square, and Sliding Bevel Square:** Combination Square is a great, accurate, 6-inch mix square, and useful for many jobs in my workshop. Jobs such as inspecting boards' squareness (when planning them to the last dimension), scribing dovetail joints, gauging the depth of mortises, and much more are done using the Combination Square.

- **Try Square**: This is used to make up workpieces for precise-fitting joints. If you're not confident about constructing your very own try square yet, you need to purchase good steel, try Square. It'll be beneficial for making square lines around the faces and sides of the boards, like a line for where to cut with your saw.

Try Square   Combination Square

Essential Power Tools

Below are the necessary power tools for a beginner to start one's projects:

Table Saw   Compound Meter Saw   Router

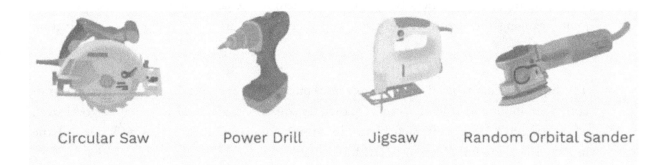

Circular Saw   Power Drill   Jigsaw   Random Orbital Sander

- **Table Saw:** A table saw is a circular saw placed under a table surface area, with a part of the blade extending through the table, where it's exposed and able to cut wood.

- **Miter Saw:** This saw is used to quickly cut crown molding, door structures, window cases, and image frames. Miter saws can also make straight cuts for general do-it-yourself (DIY) woodworking jobs. You have many options with this type of saw.

4. Woodworking Safety

> *"If you say NO safety, you would KNOW pain."*
>
> - *Noted from a Workshop Board*

Beginners' Safety Tips

1. Always put on safety gear

This may seem obvious, but it needs to be reiterated. When using loud devices like routers and surface planers, putting on ear protection is a must. Similarly, use latex gloves while doing finishes. Always wear your work goggles. These should be the first thing you grab.

Eye Safety Wear

PPE - Personal Protective Equipment

Eye protection is a must! The smallest speck in your eye, regardless of severity, can take you out for the remainder of the day.

Hearing protection, either over-ear or in-ear, provides relief with any power tools. Hearing loss is measured by the period of exposure. While it might not seem so bad at the moment, by the end of the day, your hearing will have suffered damage.

Dust masks are fantastic for avoiding the inhalation of wood dust. It might appear benign; however, timber dust is listed as a risk by safety organizations.

Handwear/Gloves may appear to be missing from this list; however, that's deliberate. While handwear covers are wonderful for many other uses, dealing with woodworking devices is not one of them. If your Handwear cover gets stuck while running a woodworking tool, it could pull your hand in with it.

Apart from PPE, other best safety practices are:
- Tying back long hair
- Removing jewelry
- Tucking in loose apparel
- Removing watches

2. Wear the right clothes

The trouble with baggy or loose garments is the risk of them getting caught in a saw blade. So, wear more well-fitted clothing. Also, remove jewelry and watches, especially anything that dangles.

3. Avoid things that adversely affect your reaction time

It's like when you're driving a vehicle: you want to avoid alcohol, drugs, and medication to prevent crashes. Never work while intoxicated. Stay safe!

4. Disconnect the power

Remember to always detach the power source itself before altering the blade orbits on your power tools. Along with ensuring the button is off, ensure that there's no power flowing to the tool.

5. Use a single expansion cable

Using one sturdy extension cable for all your power devices will verify that you turn off the power all at once. Too many cables are confusing and pose a major tripping risk.

6. Never use blunt blades &bits

Blunt tools are more dangerous to use and also make the task far more difficult in general. A well-sharpened tool will make a cleaner cut.

7. Inspect supply for existing steel

Prior to sawing or making a cut, make sure that the item doesn't have existing nails, screws, or various other pieces of steel lodged into it already. Spinning blades and nails (and various other steel) items don't mix and will trigger damages to both the stock and the cutting head. It can also cause the stock to fall apart and cause injury, so always make sure (or utilize a steel detector to guarantee for you) that the stock is tidy.

8. Work against the cutter

A lot of power devices are constructed in a manner whereby the piece of wood moves via the tool in the opposite direction. So you need to make sure that the blade or router bit cuts against the motion of the wood, as opposed to with it.

9. Never reach over a running blade

Always wait until a rotating blade has stopped moving before reaching over to get rid of waste or cut-offs and so on. To be on the safe side, remove any waste by using a push stick or scrap item.

10. Reduce interruptions

When handling interruptions, you should make sure that you finish what you were doing (finishing a cut, specifically when dealing with a power tool) before turning your attention to other places.

How to work with kids with safety: Tips for parents and caregivers

Always show the kids risk-free woodworking procedures. If you don't comply with basic safety guidelines on your own, you can't teach the same to the kids. Remember, youngsters learn from what you do, rather than say!

Make sure that the child and the tools are compatible. Additionally, make sure that both tools and job surfaces are adjusted for smaller kids. For example, confirm that the stool is adjusted to the kid's height, is steady, and unlikely to slip.

 Better yet, make your youngster a kid-sized bench-- about 26-28". Give small tools for small hands.

Describe and demonstrate safe handling methods for all devices.

Follow the time-tested best practices like don't cut towards yourself; instead, cut away from your body. Also, first, clamp the wood piece and don't hold it with another hand while cutting it.

Always monitor. Agree to set aside your very own work to assess your children as they work, specifically when they're simply discovering just how to make use of a tool.

Stand at the backside and monitor the, do not stand in front or side because it can distract the kid working on wood.

 Enable the youngster to focus entirely on what she or he is doing.

Softly correct flawed process/method verbally, but do not try to get a sharp tool out of a kid's hand in a hurry-- if you do, both of you may get hurt. Do your best to stand back and watch. Bear in mind to lock up all sharp devices when you aren't present.

Keep in mind that some power devices can hurt people without touching them. If you opt to utilize power devices-- especially the table saw, band saw, or powered sander-- while kids are present, be sure to supply ideal protection for their eyes, ears, as well as respiratory system systems.

Be honest with your youngsters (and yourself!) regarding the dangers inherent in woodworking and help them find out safe job practices early. The kids need to know precisely how to take care of tools safely as soon as they can handle them.

Parent teaching woodworking safety

5. Woodworking Projects

> *"The emotional effect of woodworking is that it gives kids that sense of accomplishment. The sheer feeling of 'Yes, I can do this!' boosts their confidence, and it spreads in all their day to day activities. Parents see a happy kid beaming with excitement of possibilities."*
>
> *-A woodworking teacher*

If you're working with your youngster while making this tool kit, it's a wonderful concept to divide the work into sessions of 45 minutes. This would avoid any loss of interest in the topic.

Let them do as much as feasible, even if it takes 10 times much longer. Generally speaking, youngsters prefer to do, rather than merely watch. Another tip is, don't sweat the details. It's okay if all the joints aren't excellent; a completed project can still make your child confident.

We have divided the projects into Easy, Intermediate, and Complex.

Let me reiterate: an adult must always give 100% focus while a kid is working on any project. The safety of the kid is the sole liability of the parent or the adult around.

Easy Projects are those where the kid can do maximum work; fewer tools are involved, and a parent is guiding at all steps and using electrical tools.

Intermediate Projects are those where kids/Teens can do a few steps, and parents do the ones involving complex steps.

Complex Projects are those where the child mainly observes or performs minimal work like applying glue, finishing, sanding, etc. The parent shows the process.

Before starting with projects, let me clarify a few points again:

- The electric tools is to be used by Parent/Guardian /Adult in charge.
- Parent/Guardian /Adult is the best judge of the steps to be carried out by kid/teen.
- You need to work in a safe environment with good lighting and a clean workspace.
- I recommend starting with some training facility/offline class where all tools are already available.

PART -1: Easy Projects

1. Pencil Holder

Materials Required

- Wood pieces

- Drill press

- Sandpaper

- Color

A pencil box holder on a working table

Instructions

- Select/cut a rectangular wood block with a length as per your requirement

Wood block and drilling

- Use a press drill for making a hole into it. You can make multiple holders by drilling various blocks one by one.

- Apply sanding on the blocks both by an electric sander and then manually using sandpaper.

Multiple wood blocks   Sanding

- Apply various colors to all the boxes. Alternatively, you can just apply some wood polish and keep the wooden texture, if you prefer.

Coloring the box   Keeping the wooden texture

2. Crayon Holder

Materials Required

- Wood pieces (2x4 piece wood suffice)

- Forstner drill bit.(1 cm hole)

- Sandpaper

- Color

- Stain/Polish

Instructions

- Select/cut a rectangular wood block with length as per your requirement

| Wood blocks | Cut and sand the wood piece |

- Cut it down to a brick shape with dimensions (length x breadth x height) 4x8x2 inches.

- Sand the wood properly with sandpaper using low grit first, followed by higher grit (300).

- Drill two lines of parallel equidistant holes as per length.

Drilling

- Apply finishing stain.

- You can color it also, as per your choice.

- Put the crayons into the holes.

Finishing Stain   Final Box

3. Small Wooden Box

Materials Required

- Wood pieces

- Forstner drill bit.(1 cm hole)

- Sandpaper

- Handsaw

- Hammer

- Nails

- Clamps

- Tape measure

- Pencils

Instructions

- Select/cut a rectangular wood block with length as per your requirement

- Adults mill stock to the density and also cut it to the lengths as the plan requires.

(Download the free plan from any of the websites mentioned in the last chapter or search "free wooden box plan" on Google).

Measure the wood   Cut to the length

- Youngsters step, mark, as well as cut the 24-in.-longboard for the long side pieces. That'll leave an item practically 6 in. long. The kids will cut it lengthwise along the saw kerf to make the board 1-3/4-inches large. Youngsters can make use of a plane to smooth the sawn edge of that piece.

- Youngsters step, mark, and also cut that 1-3/4-in.-wide board to size to make the ends.

- Kids toenail the sides throughout, being careful that the bottom edges of all the components line up.

- Youngsters cut the 10-in.-longboard to length for the bottom. They s use a plane or fining sand block to form the sides of the box base.

Planing the box base

- Kids nail the base to the box's side pieces.

- Youngsters slide the box cover in position, mark it for the preferred length, and cut it to size. Then, the kids utilize a drill with a 1/8-in. It is a little bit to make a hole for the cover stop dowel, cut the dowel to size, and fit it into the red.

- Children sand every little thing smoothly and fill it with whatever they want the box to hold.

Kid inserting the nail using hammers   Final Box after sanding

4. Bow and Arrow

<u>Materials Required</u>

- Wood pieces (1.2 m length of pine for the bow,8 mm dowel for the arrow, cotton string)
- Sandpaper
- Handsaw
- Jigsaw
- Clamps
- Tape measure
- Pencils

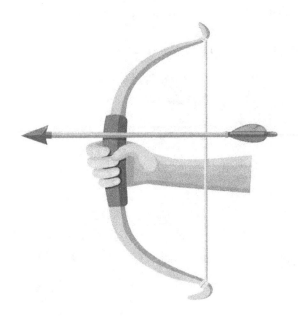

Bow and Arrow

<u>Instructions</u>

<u>Bow:</u>

- Define the bow's form by specifying the handle shape and the point at each limb's end.

- Sculpt the blank's sides to make the handle and afterward carve the tips at the end of each limb. A jigsaw or band saw would certainly expedite the procedure.

- Carve the handle to shape. You must always desire the bow's handle to be the best point; the bow flex should originate from the limbs. Leave as much timber as you can in the handle; make it comfy to hold.

- Sculpt the limbs to smooth the sides as well as lower their thickness. The thinner the limbs are, the lighter the bows pull will certainly be (as well as the less power it'll certainly have).

- Maintain the density throughout the limb to be thin progressively in the direction of the limb suggestions. Attempt to avoid hinging (where the bow bends a lot more abruptly at a weak point).

- Sculpt the nocking point at the limb pointers (where the string loops onto the limbs).

<u>Arrow</u>

- Cut the dowel to length. Try to make the arrow a few inches longer than required. Short arrowheads trigger injuries!

- Sculpt one end into a point. You can place soft points on if it's something you're worried about.

- Make use of a hand saw to cut a notch in the back of the arrowhead. This is a basic port where the string will sit when packed in the bow.

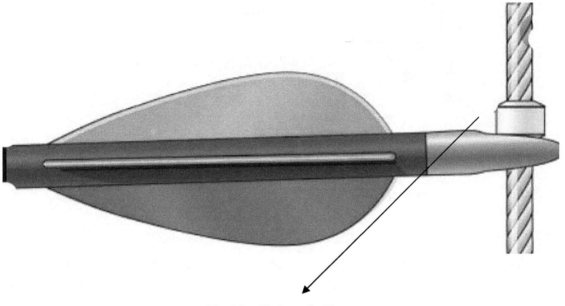

Nocking Point of a Bow

<u>String</u>

- Link a loop at one end of the cotton twine and loop it around one of the bow's nocking points.

- Bend the bow slightly and also approximate the targeted string length.

- Cut the string and link a loop at the cut end.

- String the bow and a test by pulling it back, as for the youngster would certainly simulate.

- If it feels too short or long, make a second string and repeat until you're satisfied.

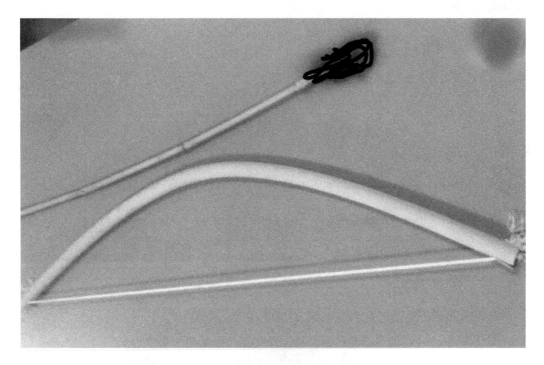

Handmade Bow and Arrow

5. Wooden Sword

Materials Required

- Wood pieces

- Sandpaper

- Handsaw/Coping Saw

- Clamps

- Tape measure

- Scissors

- Plywood

- Bond paper

- Marker/ pencil

- Epoxy

- Gray Primer/ silver and black paint

Instructions

- Draw and cut out the sword in a bond paper.

- Get hold of the bond paper as well as a pencil to make your very own layout of the sword.

- Choose how long it will be, or exactly how it ought to resemble, including all the decorations.

- Draw the sword pattern on the wood piece.

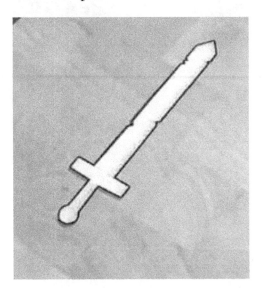

Trace the sword

- Using the pattern that you've drawn and cut, trace it onto the wood, utilize the marker to make the traces bolder.

- Cut the wooden sword along the traced line. Let the kid try this in front of you if you feel he/she is ready to use the saw.

- Sand the sword so that the ends are sharpened.

- Apply finishing polish/stain or paint it.

Use Hand Saw   Sword after sanding

6. Wooden Dog

Materials Required

- Wood piece

- Sandpaper

- Coping Saw/Jig Saw

- Pencil

- Finishing Polish

Instructions

- Draw and cut out the dog shape on a bond paper.

- Take a scrap wood piece.

- Transfer the image to the wood or stick the paper on the wood using glue.

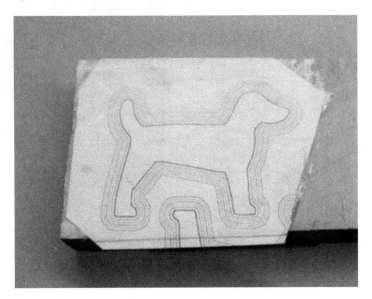

Image transfer

- Cut the dog shape using a coping saw or a jigsaw.

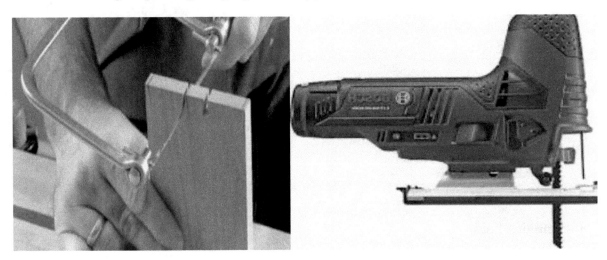

Coping Saw   Jigsaw

- Sand it and apply a wood stain/polish. Attach a rectangular base using glue.

7. Wood Mushroom

Materials Required

- Wood stick

- Sandpaper

- Coping Saw

- Carvers knife

Instructions

- Cut a stick of desired length and girth

- While wearing a glove on the hand holding the stick, start to strip away the bark to 1-1.5 cm.

Cut the wood stick

- Then with even more pressure, carve the wood into a spherical end.

- Remove much more bark: Make a decision how long you want your mushroom cap, and then strip the bark down to that level accordingly.

- Using a saw, cut a line all around to mark the end of the mushroom head. Please don't cut it too deep.

A line marking the boundary of head and cut the stem to that line

- Make Stem: Continue carving away the bark and wood to the saw line we've made in the last step. Turn the stick around while carving the stem making sure that it's thicker at the base and thinner at the top.

Wood Mushroom

- Apply sanding and finishing stain/polish of your choice.

8. Wood Pendant

<u>Materials Required</u>

- Wood piece

- Sandpaper

- Carvers knife

- Pendant bails

- Mineral Oil

- Strong coffee

- Wood cutting tools (saw, Dremel, etc.)

- Sandpaper (varying grits)

- Pliers

- Paint brush

- Rag cloth

Instructions

Use various wood types like cherry, maple, ash, etc., for different colors and select wood pieces with a fascinating grain pattern for distinct fashion jewelry.

Cut the wood piece in the desired shape you want to make the pendant.

Round Edges   Pierce a hole

Round the edges of the wood with sandpaper.

Always sand with the grain, and don't jump more than one grit size.

Pierce a hole for the bail. With a pencil, mark the pendant's center where the hole for the bail needs to go. Pierce the opening with a small bit.

Pick a natural, harmless way of discoloring the wood, coffee. Make some coffee more powerful than you'd consume. Filter it before you utilize it.

Apply the coffee tarnish with a little brush; this might take numerous coats, dry between coats. Also, lightly sand to make it smooth once again.

66

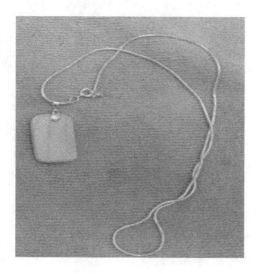

Final pendant with a string

Use mineral oil as a safe coating. It additionally deepens the shade of the wood. Put a percentage of mineral oil on a dust cloth, massage it into the wood, and rub out the extra.

Place the bail on and also squeeze it closed with pliers. Finally, add a pretty chain.

9. Wooden Fish

Materials Required

- Wood pieces

- Drill

- Clamp

- Sandpaper

- Glue

Instructions

- Select different types of woodblocks.

- Draw a fish on the flat surface.

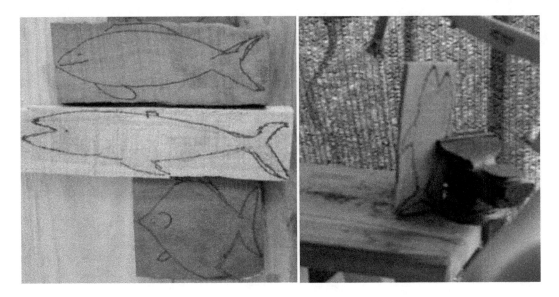

Draw a fish on the wood   Cut along the line

- Use a hack saw (for kids) to cut along the line.

- Make the mouth opening.

- Sand and color/finish.

After finishing

68

10. Wood Dice

<u>Materials Required</u>

- Wood piece (4"x4")

- Mineral Oil

- Circular Saw

- Sandpaper (varying grits)

- Paint and Brush

- Polyurethane

- Rag cloth

<u>Instructions</u>

- Cut a 4x4 inches wood piece using a circular saw.

Cut a cube wood piece   Sand it

- Sand it to make it smoother.

- Sketch the dice pips using a pencil. Make a circle using a washer, compass, or any circular object.

Sketch the pips   either apply black paint

- Use black paint or a wood-burning pen to mark the pips' black color.

Or do wood burning   Apply finishing

- Apply polyurethane coating and let it dry.

PART -2: Intermediate Projects

11. Kitchen Cutting Board

<u>Materials Required</u>

- Wood piece (durable and food safes like cherry or walnut wood)

- Sandpaper

- Mineral Oil

- Miter Saw/Circular Saw

- Drill Press

- Router

- Sandpaper (varying grits)

- Pliers

- Rag cloth

<u>Instructions</u>

- First, cut the wood piece to the desired length.

Cut the wood

- Make a hole for hanging at one of the edges as shown. (Use the hole saw on a drill press or a power drill)

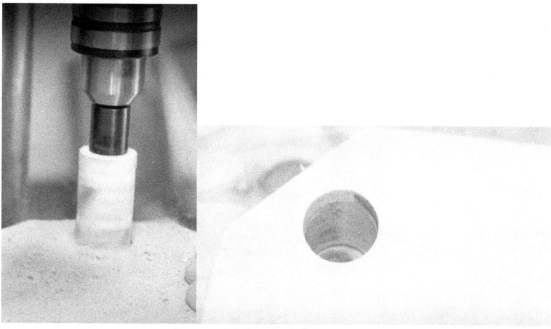

Make a hole/drill

- Now sand the board and round off the edges using a router.
- Lastly, finish it off with mineral oil, beeswax, or some other food-safe polish.

12. Wooden Puzzle

Materials Required:

- Wood Piece
- Drill
- Glue
- Measurement Tape/Ruler
- Pencil
- Scroll saw/Coping saw
- Sandpaper

Instructions:

Obtain 2 pieces of wood, 15 x 15 centimeters (MDF will do).

Draw a boundary 1 cm in from the edge on one of them and cut out the center part, leaving the only boundary.

Glue both pieces as well as clamp them. Wait until the glue is completely dry to remove the clamps.

Two-piece of MDF glued (one cutout from center)

Divide the cutout piece into different shapes to form a puzzle.

Puzzle shapes   Fit it into the base

13. Wooden Stamp

Materials Required:

- Wood Piece
- Sandpaper
- hand saw
- thumbtacks
- hammer
- nails
- drill bits
- staples

- hot glue
- different colors of acrylic paint

Instructions:

Begin by finding fallen branches. You'll utilize the hand saw to trim them right into short lengths with flat ends.

Wood Piece with flat face   Brad nails

You can use each surface for making the stamp. For instance: cover it with tacks or brad nails, as shown above, to develop polka dot stamps.

Glue for making C   Drill bit

Warm glue uses a similar impact as carving; however, in reverse. Use the gun and glue to develop a style to complete the branch or your very own set of A-B-C stamps. Drill bits, screwdriver heads, and also even threaded screws produce innovative patterns as well. Just apply the hammer to tap-tap-tap a pattern into the wood.

Nut   Stamping on paper

Use the nut on the top and provide it one solid hit afterward with a hammer or mallet. The deeper the indent in the wood, the better the marking impact in the future. The area the nut indents out to make a pattern on the wood top. Do this for all the stamps, except the screw. Place the screw on its side and hammer the side of the screw right into the timber.

You can transform your branch stump and produce an additional texture on the other side, or you can utilize them as singular stamps.

14. Growth Scale

Materials Required:

- Wood Piece
- Sandpaper
- hand saw
- Tape Measure
- Sander
- Miter Saw
- Self Stick Numbers
- Construction Square

Scale fixed to the wall

Instructions:

- Cut the wood piece as per your requirement. Measure the door where you want to put the scale.

- Pre stain the wood.

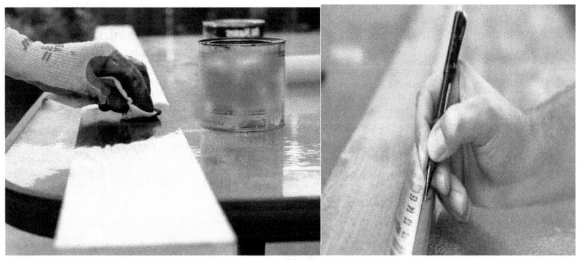

Pre Stain   Mark length

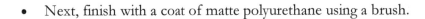

- Measure and mark the fees and inches on the woodblock using some marker.

- Next, finish with a coat of matte polyurethane using a brush.

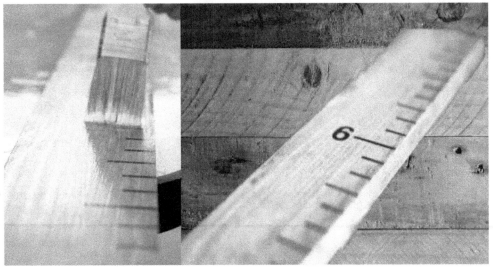

Finishing Coat   Number Sticker

- After it dries down, stick numbers of feet on the ruler. You can use a sticker or just mark it with the marker pen.

PART -3: Complex Projects

14. Wooden Balancing Board

Materials Required:

- 3 feet of 2"x4."
- Plywood: 18"x18" piece, width: 1/2 inch
- Screwdriver
- Drill
- Measurement Tape
- Pencil
- 2 ½" inch wood screws
- Saw
- Jigsaw or band saw
- Sandpaper

Instructions:

Cut three 12 inch long pieces of wood (Dimension: 2" x4")

Drawing of the Balancing Board

Utilizing a standard bucket, mark a contour on two of the pieces along the edge. Cut both rounded items with a jigsaw or a band saw.

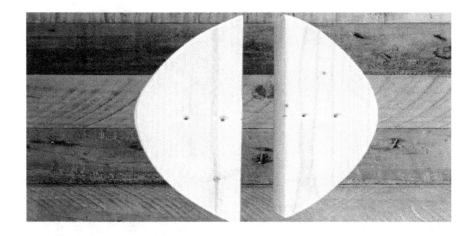

Two semicircular pieces for the base of the board

Split a quarter-inch off the one remaining wood piece. It'll serve as the center support and will require fitting enough under the curved pieces. Next, get an 18" x18" inch piece of 1/2 inch plywood.

Clamp together the curved items evenly and sand them until smooth.

The center support will go to 9 inches in the center and 3 inches from each side of the deck. Very carefully align the support item to the facility and screw it in tightly against the deck through the pilot openings from the top of the deck.

Join the centerpiece   Attach plyboard at the top with glue and screw

Align the curved pieces uniformly to the deck's sides and apply the screw to the middle of the center support wood.

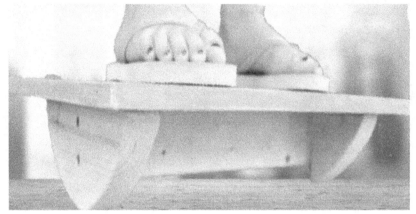

Apply finishing and color it as per the kid's choice.

15. Tool Box for Kids

Materials Required

- Wood pieces
    - 2 sides
    - 1 bottom
    - 2 ends
    - 1 handle
- Drill
- Clamp
- Sandpaper
- Glue

Instructions

Cut pieces and Connect One Side.

Cut two 1x6s as shown. Then clamp both boards with each other and utilize a 3/4" spade or Forstner drill bit to pierce the hole for the dowel. Next, affix one 1x4 side to one 1x6 end with 1-1/4" brad nails and timber adhesive.

Connect The Other Side

Connect the opposite side to one 1x6 end with 1-1/4" brad nails and timber glue.

Measuring the wood   Attaching 3 sides and bottom

Place Dowel

Squeeze some wood glue in the dowel opening and insert the 3/4" dowel, making use of a club to hammer it right into place.

Affix Other End

Squeeze some timber adhesive into the dowel hole and use a mallet to hammer the dowel right into the spot. Then make use of 1-1/4" brad nails and wood adhesive to attach the other 1x6 end.

Connect Bottom

Connect the 1/4" plywood bottom with 3/4" staples or brad nails and timber glue.

Finished Tool Box

16. Card Holder

Materials Required:

- Scrap wood (around 1" thick)
- Table saw
- Miter Saw
- Sander
- Clamps
- Glue
- Wood finish of your choice
- 1-1/4-in. brad nails
- antiskid pads
- Cotton cloth
- Rubber gloves

Instructions:

Start by measuring as well as cutting your wood to 12" in size.

Wood piece

Then run the wood item through the table saw long-ways at 1".

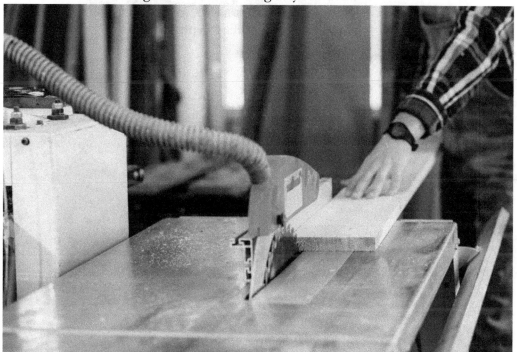

Cut the wood using the saw

Set the table saw blade at 10 degrees and lower it to an elevation that will cut about halfway via your wood.

Make the card holding depth

Sand and apply a finishing coat.

Sand and Finish

Final Card Holder

17. Comb

<u>Materials Required:</u>

- Scrap wood
- Jigsaw
- Sandpaper
- Beeswax

<u>Instructions:</u>

- Prepare the Wood

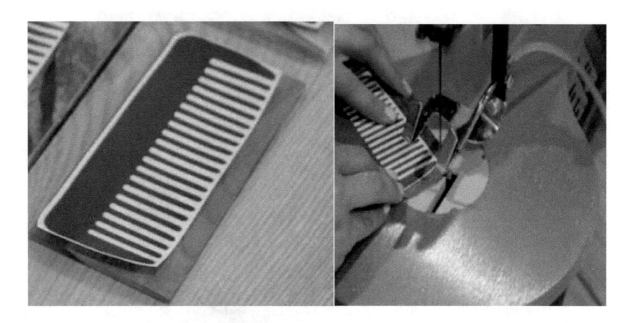

Draw on paper   Jig Saw

Select the lumber you want to use for this task and prep it by cutting it to size. Run the wood through the planner to get the desired thickness.

- Sand

Next, sand your item to the preferred thickness of your comb.

- Apply Your Layout/comb design

When your piece has been sanded and cut to its dimension, use a stencil of the shape you would like to cut your comb. You can find the stencils on Google by searching "Comb Clip Art" and then attach the patterns using a spray adhesive.

- Cutting& Forming the Combs

Cut the combs using a scroll saw or jigsaw. Next, sand, form, and fine-tune your combs. You need to work between sanding and engraving bits on a rotary tool to achieve the final shape.

- Complete the Comb.

After your pieces have been formed, sand the item to 400 grit and complete it with a finishing coat.

18. Chess Board

Materials Required :

-
- Light and dark wood pieces
- Table saw
- Sander
- Clamps
- Glue
- Wood finish of your choice

Finished Chess Board

Instructions:

For the wood, it's more effective to pick two species of a comparable firmness, such as the oak as well as the mahogany I employed. Maple is also great for the lighter timber.

Wood pieces

The first step is to cut eight strips of timber, four of each color. The strips must determine the size of two inches (or whatever you choose for the square dimension) by at the very least 20 inches. A table saw is most likely to give you the best opportunity at accuracy as well as consistency. Use of a round saw is essential, but you'll want to set up some straight side to run the saw against. Lay the strips in an alternating pattern (dark and light).

Apply glue and clamp it

Choose one side to be the top face (the side you'll see when the board is complete). Once they're organized in a way that you enjoy, I suggest numbering the strips, which will undoubtedly be a useful reference guide once the gluing begins.

Ensure to spread out the glue equally along the whole edge of each strip. It's essential that the gluing is done appropriately, or points can fall apart in the future.

The clamps must be completely perpendicular to the board's edges so they don't do any damages.

When the adhesive has dried, it's time to cut 2-inch strips from the board you just made. This time, make the cuts vertical to the original strips.

If you're utilizing a table saw, run the squared-off side along the fence. Since you began with 20-inch strips of the raw material, this will certainly leave you with at least nine checkerboard strips.

Cut them and then glue again to get the 64 alternate square patterns

Take those strips, each of which includes 8 even squares. Then lay them out once again, this moment turning every other one.

When the adhesive has dried, unclamp the board and sand it smooth.

For a nice, finished look, include a border. Lastly, apply whatever surface you like to your board.

Clamp it   Apply finishing

Final Chess Board

19. Tic- Tac- Toe Board Game

Caution/Note: This project is a bit complicated and involves using a lathe; parents should do the maximum work on the machines. Kids should perform simpler steps. In case you don't have a lathe, use a whittling knife on softwood to do the same (Doing this could actively involve the kid).

Materials Required

While any woods will work, I advise three types of timber for the job:
- Light Maple
- Oak
- Black Walnut.

Make use of the maple for the trim, the oak for the blocks, and the walnut for the strips. Also, a hand-rubbed linseed oil finish brings out the grains.

Tools:

- Paper, Pen, Set Square
- Wood Piece for Board and scrap wood for O's and X's
- Band Saw, Jigsaw, and Lathe for Wood Turning
- Danish Oil, Sanding Tool

Instructions

- Make 2" squares for Crosses.

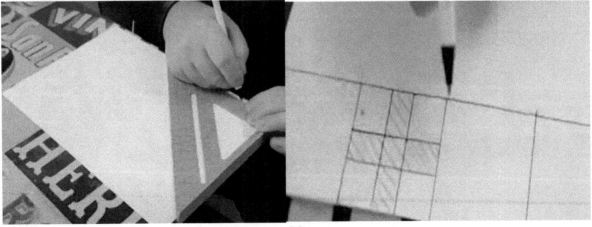

96

2" square master Cross

- Cut the crosses. Take out the scrap wood from any firewood pile and cut to size, as shown below (for making X's). Cut the wood strip on the band saw.

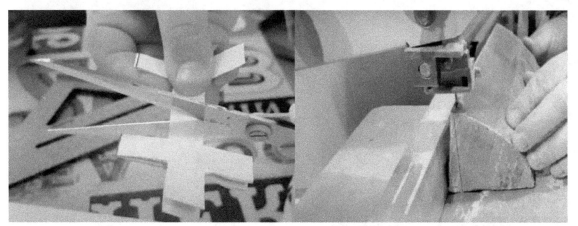

Paper Crosses   Cut strip of Band Saw

- Now, stick the paper template on the wood. Make O's by turning the lathe.

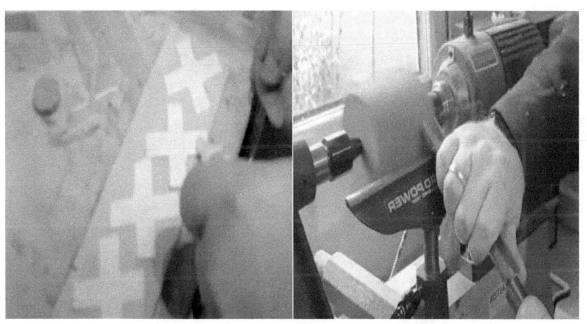

Carving X

- Drill the hole and then cut the slices of the cylindrical wood piece.

Carving O

- Now cut the crosses which were stuck on the wood piece earlier (using jigsaw). Then sand the X pieces.

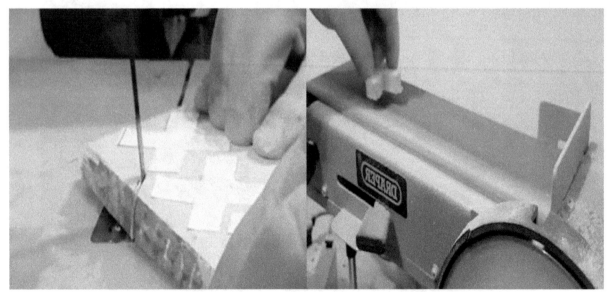

Using Jigsaw

- After sanding, put a coat of Danish oil on the X's and O's and cut out the board. Sand the board and spray white color.

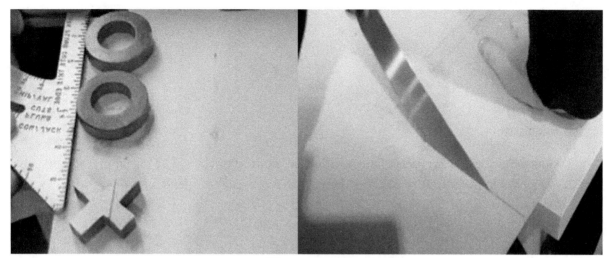

X's and the O's

- Draw boxes on the whiteboard and then put the X's and the O's.

Tic Toe Board

20. Candle Holder

<u>Materials Required</u>

- Wood: Find some scrap pieces/sheets of wood, not too thick (< 1/2" is simpler to cut). You need to have at least two colors (better three or more) to blend with plywood.
- Wood adhesive
- Forstner bit: To drill the hole for the required candle size
- Power drill
- A saw: Jig or Table Saw
- Sanding block
- Sandpaper: 60, 100, and 200 (or comparable grits).
- Clearcoat and a paint shrub
- Setsquare
- A vice will certainly be valuable but isn't necessary
- Some clamps are also helpful but not essential

<u>Instructions</u>

Dimension Planning
- Ask yourself exactly how big/tall you want the holders and see what dimension the scrap wood permits.
- For example, you can make them square, about 3" x 3", if the candles are 1 1/2" in size.
-

Cut the wood
- Begin by making a pattern out of the cardboard.
- Then use the pattern to trace equal squares on each item of wood.
- Now you cut the wood: use your saw or power tools to cut the squares.
- After you've cut the timber, don't sand the edges yet; gluing comes first.

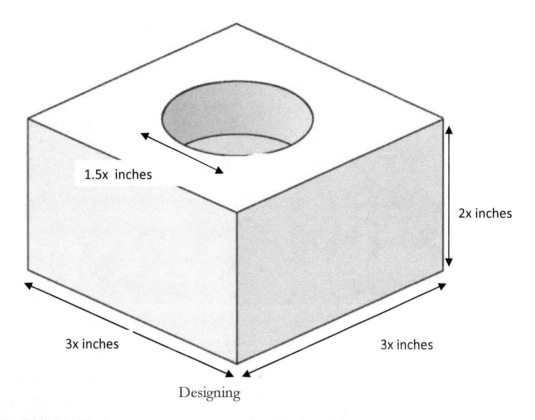

1.5x inches

2x inches

3x inches

3x inches

Designing

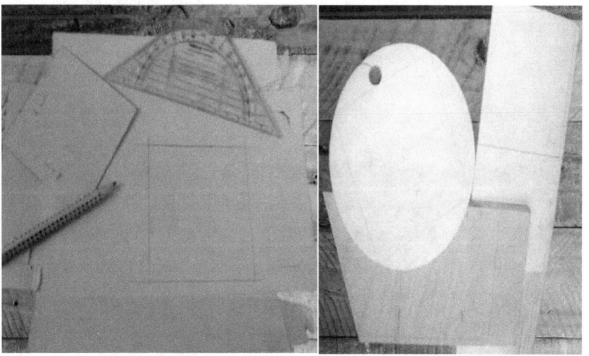

Cut the square

Gluing

- Cut the squares of the desired color; glue them together - on top of each other.
- The glue should be applied in optimum quantity. Both too much and/or too little glue will impact the strength of the bond negatively.

Gluing

Sanding

- Relying on how exactly you cut the timber, this process can be really quick or rather slow.
- You start with the roughest paper on the sanding-block to make the four side surface areas flat; after that, switch to the medium sandpaper and go over the same surfaces.
- While sanding, always check if you have right angles. Likewise, do that with a set square. Mark the areas where you need to grind even more timber off and do it.
- Use the finest paper to make all the surfaces and sides smooth.

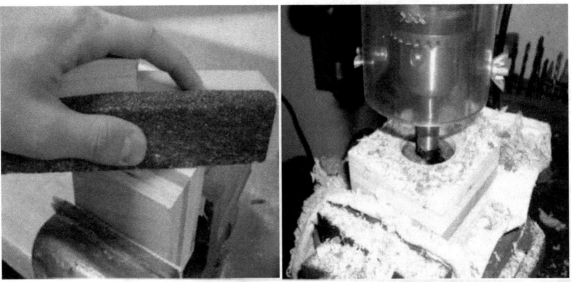
Sanding and Drilling

Drilling

- Attach the Forstner bit to your drill.
- Make two diagonal lines and locate the center on topmost Square.
- If you only have a hand drill, take extreme care to hold it as upright as feasible, look from different directions to examine if you are.
- After that, use the fine sandpaper again to smooth the edge of the hole.

Paint

- Use a paintbrush to add the clear layer to the timber - read the instructions on the can/bottle to know when it's completely dry.
- When the initial layer of clear coat is completely dry, utilize 400 sandpaper to smooth the surface areas once more; after that, apply an additional layer of clear coat.
- Let it dry once again.
- You're officially done!

Finishing and final candle holder

6. Final Tips and Conclusion

> *"Measure Twice and Cut Once."*- English Proverb

So, how did you find the book to this point? I hope you've gained an overall picture of woodworking scope, processes, and tools.

It's a very vast topic with many sub-niches inside it. The practitioners start with a generic approach and specialize in a particular genre of woodworking.

Before concluding, I'd like to discuss a few more critical points about *How to practice woodworking safely while you are starting.* It's like if you'd have attended Woodworking class since we offer comprehensive instructions, similar to what you would have acquired in the first few classes!

At the beginning of my woodworking journey, I attended a few preparatory classes. A few lessons remained with me for a long time, as noted below:

Tips for woodworking with kids and teens:

- Let youngsters dive in as well as create a completed job. Don't get fixated with teaching higher level woodworking strategies beyond the fundamentals needed for the specific session.
- Stick to minor tools required for the task; prep and layout all materials, and be prepared to go.
- Maintain each process in short intervals, under a few minutes.
- If a youngster loses interest, don't force the child and let them take a break.
- Concentrate on assembling instead of cutting timber. Work with pre-cut pieces also.

Friend and Enemy Concept

Friend

- Good Lighting
- Clean working area
- Good Ventilation
- Clean finishing applicators(Rags and Brushes)
- Safety Gears

Enemy

- Saw Dust
- Messy working area
- Sloppy Stainers
- Distraction while using power tool

Instructions before starting with any project

- Plan beforehand and then work as per your plan; avoid going with the flow methodology. Visualize it before taking the tools. Always rehearse cuts until you're fully confident.
- Embrace the golden rule, "Measure twice or thrice before cutting once."
- Always be focused while using tools. Lack of concentration or any kind of distractions can cause injury.
  Before starting, look for knots or nails in the wood and also avoid using green lumber.
- Don't use your hand to clean up the sawdust, shavings, and scrap material; use a hand brush instead.
- Keep your cell phone off or on mute. Avoid distractions while using any tool.
- While lifting, don't strain yourself and always keep your back straight.
- Finishing material is highly combustible or prone to catch fire. So use them safely, and be sure to keep them away from and hot tool or flame. The same tips apply to rugs and brushes.

Using power tools safely

The first safety tip I got was: ***The safety of the tool is dependent on your focus.***

Below are the basic safety tips for using woodworking tools:

- Always keep machine guards in place.
- Remember to have a proper wood size for a cut. A bigger or smaller one can cause an accident.
- Learn proper hand placement: Hold the wood firmly; don't push wood hard towards the blade.
- Watch your fingers and keep them clear.
- ***Golden Rule: Sharper tools are safe than dull ones.*** Dull tools require extra pressure, which causes slips and accidents.
- Lastly, learn to engage all your senses with the craft.

Tips for Getting Started

- Create a simple woodworking setup to start.
- Make sure you understand how to take tape measurements.
- Master basic lumber measurements and types.
- Only use straight wood boards to begin.
- Start with just the essential tools.
- Sand, sand, and sand your wood some more!
- Identify the wood's moisture content before starting any work.
- Keep your workshop clean and well-lit.
- Maintain sharp tools.

Safety Tips

- Always remember that the safe way is the right way!
- Learn how to operate tools before using them safely.
- Make sure all safety equipment is properly functioning before starting.
- Ensure that the tool's exhaust system is working correctly.
- Don't reach through any moving machine components.
- Don't talk to others while operating tools.
- Don't force anything into the machine.

- Turn the tool off entirely before removing blockages.
- After switching off the power, don't attempt to stop blades or edges from moving with a stick or your hand.
- Know where all emergency switches are.
- Don't play with tools or equipment: they aren't toys
- Use approved eye protection.
- Get first aid for any cut or scratch, no matter how minor.

Guidelines

Guidelines for parents/adult:
1. Set a positive example of a caring craft.
2. Supervise the kids, answer inquiries, and show them how to utilize tools securely.
3. Mill wood to density, according to the cut list. Make any preliminary cuts as specified in the instructions and also make extra components to permit errors.
4. Leave task designs open for kids to test their concepts, develop issues independently, and find proactive solutions. Please encourage them to find and examine their remedies.
5. Be a cheerleader and coach for their work.
6. Praise the children for a job well done and specify the feedback.

Guidelines for youngsters
1. Pay close attention to what the adults tell you.
2. Ask a lot of questions.
3. Constantly use devices specifically as you're told.
4. Enjoy.

Rules for functioning with safety
1. No woodworking without adult guidance.
2. No playing around in the work area.
3. Use clamps or a bench vise to hold when cutting, sanding.
4. When using a saw, either hold it with both hands and place one hand behind your back.

Conclusion: Woodwork is worth the effort. Every child and teen needs to have these sensational experiences! It is a pure joy to see children engrossed so deeply. You'll be surprised by the depth of youngsters' involvement and also the breadth of their overall creativity. Observing their imagination and problem-solving skill at work will certainly raise your spirits, promote digital detox, and foster DIY projects at home!

This concludes our discussion. I hope you liked the content. I'd sincerely appreciate it if you could share your feedback and reviews on the platform. You can also reach me at valueadd2life@gmail.com.

Practice safely!

Respectfully,

Stephen Fleming

7. Appendix

Appendix 1: Woodworking Glossary

- Adhesive: A material that is capable of bonding products together when added to a surface. Glue and contact cement are examples

- Abrasive: Any of the layered papers, textiles, or various other products (including pumice, rottenstone, as well as steel woolen) utilized for smoothing timber or between-coat smoothing of surfaces.

- Acetone - An anemic liquid solvent typically used for cleansing surfaces and the removal of paint and finishes.

- Adze - An axe-like device used to form and appear timber, as well as lumber.

- Aliphatic resin glue - A solid and quick-drying adhesive, more commonly called timber adhesive or woodworker's glue.

- Ampere - A unit of dimension for the electrical present, commonly seen in its abbreviated form as amps.

- Apron - The portion of a table that connects the surface of the tabletop to the legs.

- Arbor - A pin or shaft on which a tool can be connected, such as a router bit or table saw blade.

- Architect's rule (n) - Also referred to as an architect's scale, a triangular ruler with units of measurement marked on each edge.

- Backsaw (n) - A hand saw with an inflexible rib along the rear of the blade, opposite the cutting edge, to avoid bending as well as enable a steady sawing process.

- Band saw (n) - Type of a power saw that makes use of a toothed steel blade in a continuous or looped set.

- Bar clamp (n) - A type of clamp with a lengthy bar that extends two clamping jaws, used to hold large products.

- Basswood (n) - A soft, fine wood frequently utilized in sculpting.

- Bevel (v) – Used to cut a piece of timber to a sloped edge; (n)-- an angled piece of timber cut to a dimension besides 90 degrees.

- Biscuit (n) - A small slice of timber is put into holes or ports into timber items, therefore joining the two.

- Butt joint (n) - A basic, however weak, woodworking joint, generally established as end-grain-to-face-grain, end-grain-to-long-grain, or long-grain-to-long grain.

- Cabinet saw (n) - An industrial-grade table saw, usually consisting of a large motor and trunnion pins attached and an enclosed base.

- Cabinetmaker (n) -   A professional woodworker that develops beautiful furniture.

- Compound miter saw (n) - This is a power miter saw that rotates on an axis and the arm. Some compound miter saws, called sliding compound miter saws, slide along rails.

- Deal (v) - The process of fixing two pieces of timber together by sawing an adverse profile of one into the other with a favorable account; a term is frequently used in molding.

- Crosscut - This refers to any cut made with a vertical positioning to the grain of the wood, the act of making such a cut, and the wood that has been cut in such a manner.

- Cutting checklist (n) - An extensive list of the products required to complete a task, consisting of the names of the needed pieces as well as the measurements of each item: in some cases, a diagram of the boards is needed.

- Drawknife (n) - This is a type of blade with a handle on both ends.

- Engineer's Square (n) - Used for showing 90 degrees, it refers to an accurate steel square with a fixed blade.

- Forstner bit (n) - A tool used to create tidy, flat-bottomed, and also frequently larger holes.

- Grain (n) - Qualities of a timber piece that describe its appearance, figuring, or porosity.

110

- Groove (n) -A three-sided trench cut into a wood board that is made along the grain.

- Hacksaw (n) - A handsaw, often used for cutting steels, that has a handle at one end and holds at both ends.

- Hand plane (n) - A cutting device used for cutting timber with a blade kept in the area at a steep angle. Hand planes can come in many varieties, including block, bench, bull nose, spokes have, router, scrape, and also rabbet hand planes.

- Jigsaw (n) - A powered, upright, reciprocating blade, used for cutting various products relying on the type of blade utilized. It is called a jigsaw, as it can cut jigsaw puzzles.

- Joinery (n) - The act of connecting pieces of wood with each other. This can be completed in various ways, such as using glue and mechanical fasteners or, more typically, by interlacing matching wooden joints.

- Kerf (n) - The excess wood removed by a saw blade in between the timber item and the off cut.

- Kickback (n), unwind (v) - The reverse action seen in woodworking machines when they throw a work surface back in the operator's direction.

- Lap joint (n) - A joint made use of to enhance a frame edge. Located at either the corner (end lap), in the middle of one piece (T-lap), or in the middle of 2 items (X-lap), it deals extra toughness than an enhanced joint, but is weaker than a mortise-and-tenon joint.

- Medium-density fiberboard (n) - Abbreviated MDF, an engineered panel product, including wood fibers, that are glued under warmth and pressure.

- Miter (n) - The surface area that develops a joint's beveled edge.

- Miter Saw (n) - A power saw that cuts miters, similar to a circular saw.

- Orbital sander (n) - A sander that makes use of the motor's power to develop minute circles, which allows the sandpaper to abrade a surface area.

- Planer (n) - A power device used to plane wood or make the wood piece plane as per the required thickness.

- Points per inch (adj) - A means to identify saw blades (shortened "ppi").

111

- Rabbet (n, v) - A trench cut into the side of a board that is made up of two-sides.

- Rabbet joint (n) - A basic joint for box structure, allowing for more strength than a butt joint by adding an extra gluing surface area that secures against racking.

- Table saw (n) - A stationary, arbor-driven round saw that is housed below the table in which the workpiece is cut.

- Tenon (n, v) - A rabbeted side that is utilized by insertion into a matching recess, commonly called a mortise.

- Wedge (n) - A small, cut item of wood that is secured in a cut slit in the long run of a predicting item of timber, referred to as a through-tenon.

Appendix 2: Adhesives Chart

ADHESIVES CHART

MATERIALS→	Paper	Fabric	Felt	Leather	Rubber	Foam	Styrofoam	Plastic	Metal	Ceramic	Glass	Balsa	Cork	Wood
Wood	W	C/W	Sp/C	W/C/Ca	C/Ca	C	2K/H	L/C	2K/C/L	C/Ca	C/Ca	W	W	L/W
Cork	H/W	H/L	W	Ca/C	Ca/C	2K	W	L/Ca	C/Ca	L/Ca	Si	W	W	
Balsa	W	H/W	W	Ca/C	C/Ca	C	2K/H	L/Ca	2K/Ca	L/Ca	C/Ca	W		
Glass	A/W	A	A	A/Ca	Ca	Sp	2K/Sp	C/L	2K/C	2K/C/L	2K/L			
Ceramic	A/H	Ca/A	Ca/A	Ca/A/C	C/Ca	A	Ce/C	L/Ca/C	2K/C/L	Ce/Ca				
Metal	A/H	A	C	C/Ca	C/Ca	C	2K/H	2K/C	2K/C					
Plastic	H/Sp	Sp/C	Sp/C	Sp/Ca	C/Ca	Ca	Ca/C	L/Ca/2K						
Styrofoam	Sp/C	A/H	Sp	A	L	L/A	A/Sp							
Foam	Sp	Sp	Sp	C	C	Sp								
Rubber	Ca/C	A/C	C	Ca	Ca									
Leather	F/Sp	F	2K	C/F										
Felt	A/H	F/H	H/F											
Fabric	A/H	F/H												
Paper	A/W													

Legend:

- **A** All-purpose-glue
- **F** Fabric glue
- **Sp** Spray adhesive
- **H** Hot glue
- **C** Contact adhesives
- **L** Construction adhesive (Liquid Nails, Loctite)
- **Ce** Ceramic glue
- **Si** Silicone
- **W** Wood glue
- **Ca** Cyanoacrylate (super glue)
- **2K** Two-component adhesive

Appendix 3: Sources of Free Design/Layout/Project Ideas

1. https://www.rockler.com/free-woodworking-plans

2. https://www.woodsmithplans.com/free-plans/

3. https://www.thesprucecrafts.com/free-woodworking-plans-for-your-home-and-yard-1357146

4. https://www.canadianwoodworking.com/free-plans

5. https://www.finewoodworking.com/blog/free-woodworking-plans

Other Books in DIY Series

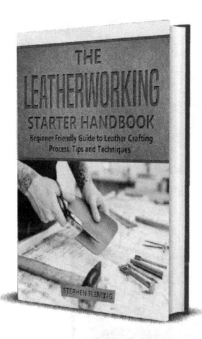

We'd Love Your Feedback!

Please let us know how we're doing by leaving us a review.

CPSIA information can be obtained
at www.ICGtesting.com
Printed in the USA
BVHW010847181021
619199BV00015B/409